THE SONGS OF
Hugh Martin
From Broadway to Hollywood and the West End

EDITORS:

Judy Bell • The Richmond Organization

Paul Christman • The University of Oklahoma

ISBN 978-1-4234-5896-8

Cromwell Music, Inc.

 The Richmond Organization

EXCLUSIVELY DISTRIBUTED BY

7777 W. BLUEMOUND RD. P.O. BOX 13819 MILWAUKEE, WI 53213

Visit Hal Leonard Online at
www.halleonard.com

Special Thanks: Daniel Carne, Fred and Elaine Harrison, Michael McGinnis, Terry O'Donnell, Howard Richmond

Photo Credits: Photofest (pages 6, 27, 84, 124), remaining photos from the collections of Hugh Martin and Paul Christman

CONTENTS

THE STORY OF MY LIFE

Birmingham, Alabama was an odd place for a musician to be born. We're quite cultured now in the 21st century, but in 1914, when I came on the scene, Birmingham was all steel mills, iron foundries and coal mines. It was the year of *The Guns of August,* that famous book by Barbara Tuchman about the outbreak of World War I, not only the year, but the very month.

I was born in a Victorian style residence that looks (it's still there) a lot like the Smith home in *Meet Me in St. Louis.* I loved Birmingham and my beautiful happy family, also not unlike the idyllic Smith family of the movie. But, although I had the best of training at Phillips High School, Birmingham-Southern College, and the Birmingham Conservatory of Music, I couldn't keep my mind on science, sociology, or sonatas. My mother was in love with New York, and her love for that 'city with no heart' (as it's called in Warner Brothers movies) 'contaged' itself to me.

I dropped out of college after a year of daydreaming about skyscrapers and bright lights and theaters with my name on their marquees. I didn't know whether I was an arranger or a pianist or an actor. The one thing I never thought of being was a songwriter, though the music of Gershwin and Kern was a tremendous influence on me.

That exciting way of making a living hit me as a total surprise in 1941. I was twenty-seven years old when a show I had written with Ralph Blane, *Best Foot Forward*, opened on Broadway. Overnight the show was a hit, and Ralph and I were hailed by all nine of the New York theater critics as a bright new team of Tin Pan Alleyites.

Top L to R: Hugh Martin and Ralph Blane
Bottom L to R: Jo Jean Rogers and Phyllis Rogers

We got the job, miraculously, by entering a contest, the single judge being Richard Rodgers. He was half of Rodgers and Hart then, and would eventually become half of Rodgers and Hammerstein when Lorenz Hart died in 1943. I had an inside track with Dick Rodgers because in 1938 he had assigned me to do the vocal arrangement of "Sing for Your Supper" for his and Larry's *The Boys from Syracuse*.

Shortly after *Best Foot Forward* opened, MGM offered Ralph and me a seven-year contract. We were reluctant to accept it because, with Phyllis Rogers and her sister Jo Jean Rogers, we (Ralph and I) had been singing happily as The Martins Quartet. We were featured on Broadway in *Louisiana Purchase*, a show by Irving Berlin and with Fred Allen on his national radio series Texaco Star Theatre.

But we decided to travel west and soon our Hollywood good fortune exceeded our New York good fortune. In addition to putting *Best Foot Forward* on film, Arthur Freed and Roger Edens gave Ralph and me a plum assignment: writing three new songs for Judy Garland to sing in *Meet Me in St. Louis*. The movie was a huge success, so much so that it gave our three new songs a gratifying push. They were "The Trolley Song", "The Boy Next Door", and "Have Yourself a Merry Little Christmas".

Almost a decade later in 1951, Judy Garland invited me to share with her the stage of the Palace Theatre as her accompanist. In that mecca of vaudeville, we did 'two a day' for nineteen weeks. She was a tremendous musician and the greatest talent I've ever encountered in my life.

During those 'Golden Years' of Broadway and Hollywood Musicals, I wrote music and lyrics for five stage shows and contributed songs to five films. God blest me mightily with those shows, including *Love from Judy* for which Timothy Gray and I wrote the songs. It ran for a year and a half at the Saville Theatre in London's West End. Tim and I also had a Broadway hit in 1964, *High Spirits*, adapted from Noël Coward's comedy *Blithe Spirit*.

Sounds like an effortless climb up the ladder of success, doesn't it? It wasn't! There were a lot of flops, too, but many of them contained songs that were worth salvaging, some of which are included in this folio. About my output of songs, I always think of the famous line Spencer Tracy spoke about Katharine Hepburn in *Pat and Mike*: "There's not much of her, but what there is is cherce!"

Let me balance the ledger by telling you a little about the dark side of show biz. In 1960, I had a nervous breakdown in London—big time. It should have been the worst possible news. Actually, it was the best possible news because it led directly to my becoming born again. In 1974, my faith in God and Jesus Christ became the most important thing in my life, and it still is.

From 1994 to 2004 I worked on a memoir, tentatively called *Hugh Who?* I finally finished it in 2004, the year I turned ninety. I can't believe everything that's happened to me. All my dreams have come true. Everything I've ever wanted, God has given me. In a sense, "the story of my life" is the songs you will find between the covers of this folio—a story that might never have been told but for the loving persistence of my friends Judy Bell and Paul Christman.

Hugh Martin

BEST FOOT FORWARD

(1941, 1943)

Hugh Martin and Ralph Blane's first musical, *Best Foot Forward*, concerned teenagers preparing for a prom at a Pennsylvania prep school. The young songwriting team created a vibrant score for the youthful story, including the spirited march "Buckle Down Winsocki" and the sentimental ballad "Ev'ry Time." Two years after its Broadway debut, MGM released the film version of *Best Foot Forward*, keeping seven of the original songs and adding three new ones by Martin and Blane. The musical was televised on the NBC *Oldsmobile Saturday Spectaculars* in 1954, revived Off-Broadway in 1963 and produced by the York Theatre in 2004.

New York run: October 1, 1941 – July 4, 1942
(Ethel Barrymore Theatre, 326 performances)
Music & lyrics: Hugh Martin & Ralph Blane
Book: John Cecil Holm
Producer: George Abbott
(Richard Rodgers uncredited)
Director: George Abbott
Choreographer: Gene Kelly
Conductor: Archie Bleyer
Orchestrations: Donald Walker & Hans Spialek
(Overture by Robert Russell Bennett)
Scenery & lighting: Jo Mielziner
Costumes: Miles White

Gil Stratton, Jr. and Rosemary Lane

Cast: Rosemary Lane *(Gale Joy)*; Marty May *(Jack Haggerty)*; Gil Stratton, Jr. *(Bud Hooper)*; Maureen Cannon *(Helen Schlessinger)*; Nancy Walker *(Blind Date)*; June Allyson *(Minerva)*; Kenneth Bowers *(Hunk Hoyt)*; Victoria Schools *(Ethel)*; Tommy Dix *(Chuck Green)*; Lee Roberts *(Goofy Clark)*; Danny Daniels *(Junior)*; Jack Jordan, Jr. *(Dutch Miller)*; Lou Wills, Jr. *(Fred Jones)*; Richard Dick *(Freshman)*; Bobby Harrell *(Satchel Moyer)*; Fleming Ward *(Dr. Reeber)*; Stuart Langley *(Old Grad)*; Betty Anne Nyman *(Miss Ferguson)*; Roger Hewlett *(Professor Lloyd)*; Norma Lehn *(Waitress)*; Vincent York *(Chester Billings)*; Robert Griffith *(Prof. Williams)*

Songs (by Martin unless noted): Don't Sell the Night Short; Three Men on a Date (lyrics by Blane); That's How I Love the Blues; The Three B's; Ev'ry Time; The Guy Who Brought Me (music & lyrics by Richard Rodgers & Martin); I Know You by Heart; Shady Lady Bird (music & lyrics by Blane); Buckle Down, Winsocki (music & lyrics-Blane); My First Promise (music & lyrics-Blane); What Do You Think I Am; Just a Little Joint with a Jukebox; Where Do You Travel? (music & lyrics-Blane); I'd Gladly Trade; The Old Hollywood Story*; A Raving Beauty*; You Are for Loving*; Up to My Eyebrows**

*added to the 1963 Off-Broadway revival (Liza Minnelli's stage debut)
**added to the 2004 York Theatre revival

CD: Varèse Sarabande (1963 Off-Broadway revival cast)

At the Winsocki prom, Kenny Bowers (left) and Tommy Dix (in hat) greet movie star Lucille Ball, who played herself in the film.

Film premiere: New York, June 1943 (93 minutes)
Music & lyrics: Hugh Martin & Ralph Blane
Screenplay: Irving Brecher & Fred Finklehoffe (from the Broadway musical by Martin, Blane & Holm)
Producer: Arthur Freed (MGM)
Director: Edward Buzzell
Choreographer: Charles Walters
Music Director: Lennie Hayton
Orchestrations: Conrad Salinger, Jack Matthias, LeRoy Holmes, George Bassman & Leo Arnaud
Recording Director: Douglas Shearer
Cinematography: Leonard Smith (Technicolor)
Film Editor: Blanche Sewell
Art Director: Cedric Gibbons
Set Decoration: Edwin B. Willis
Costumes: Irene Sharaff
Makeup: Jack Dawn

Cast: Lucille Ball *(Lucille Ball,* vocal by Gloria Grafton*)*; William Gaxton *(Jack O'Riley)*; Virginia Weidler *(Helen Schlessinger)*; Tommy Dix *(Bud Hooper)*; Nancy Walker *(Blind Date)*; June Allyson *(Minerva Pierce)*; Kenny Bowers *(Dutch Miller)*; Gloria DeHaven *(Ethel)*; Jack Jordan *(Hunk Hoyt)*; Beverly Tyler *(Miss Delaware Water Gap)*; Chill Wills *(Chester Short)*; Henry O'Neill *(Major Reeber)*; Donald MacBride *(Capt. Bradd)*; Sara Haden *(Miss Talbott)*; Darwood Kaye *(Killer)*; Bob Stebbins *(Greenie)*; Morris Ankrum *(Col. Harkrider)*; Nana Bryant *(Mrs. Dalyrimple)*; Harry James & His Music Makers

Songs (by Martin unless noted): Wish I May, Wish I Might; Three Men on a Date (lyrics by Blane); Two O'Clock Jump (Harry James, Count Basie & Benny Goodman); Ev'ry Time; Flight of the Bumble Bee (Rimsky-Korsakov); The Three B's; I Know You by Heart; Shady Lady Bird (Blane); My First Promise (Blane); Alive and Kicking (Martin & Blane); You're Lucky; Buckle Down, Winsocki (Blane)

CD: Rhino Handmade (Soundtrack)
DVD: Warner Home Video

Ev'ry Time

*Sacred Words by
HUGH MARTIN

Words and Music by
HUGH MARTIN and RALPH BLANE

Slowly

mp

cresc.

f *rit. e dim.*

Verse

5 B♭maj7 B♭m6 Am7 A♭dim

False or true?_____ I wish I had a clue or two_____ Where I stood I

p a tempo

9 Gm7 Caug Fmaj7 D9 G9 C7susA

thought I knew_____ or should._____

cresc. *rit. e. dim.*

13 B♭maj7 B♭m6 Am7 A♭dim

True or false?_____ Life was a nev-er end-ing waltz_____ Then it caught the

a tempo

* *Dedicated to Del Decker*

"Ev'ry Time"

Second Refrain

Ev'ry time I feel a little brave,
I always get a little scare.
Ev'ry time I want a little bone,
I always find the cupboard bare.

Ev'ry time I play a little golf,
I'm always over par.
Ev'ry time I sail my little boat,
She's never very yar.

Ev'ry time I feel a little warm,
I always catch a little cold.
Ev'ry time I feel a little young,
I always grow a little old.

And when I build my cabin in the sky,
It tumbles from its mark.
Leaving just a lonely lady in the dark.

Act II Reprise

Ev'ry time I try to be a help,
I always take it on the chin.
Ev'ry time I hurry to the rescue,
Always get a Mickey Finn.

Ev'ry time I play a little gin,
I'm always short an ace.
Ev'ry time I sign a little check,
It bounces in my face.

Ev'ry time I buy a little stock,
It always takes a little drop.
Ev'ry time I think I've got a hit,
I always get a little flop.

And when I think my name will be in lights,
It dwindles to a spark.
Leaving just a lonely little lady in the dark.

The Martins Quartet (L to R: Ralph Blane, Phyllis Rogers, Jo Jean Rogers and Hugh Martin)

You're Lucky

Words and Music by
HUGH MARTIN and RALPH BLANE

Refrain—Slowly with Expression

What Do You Think I Am

Words and Music by
HUGH MARTIN and RALPH BLANE

FOR ME AND MY GAL (1942)
"Three Cheers for the Yanks" (music & lyrics: Hugh Martin)

In this MGM sentimental WWI era story, Judy Garland, George Murphy and Gene Kelly played aspiring vaudeville artists. Asked to write a song for the movie, Hugh adapted a 'trunk' song of his "We've Done It Before, We Can Do It Again" into "Three Cheers for the Yanks." However, the song was eventually cut from the film. An outtake of the number is included on the compact disc, performed by Judy Garland with Six Hits and a Miss.

Film premiere: New York, October 1942 / Los Angeles, November 1942 (104 minutes)
CD: Rhino (Soundtrack)
DVD: Warner Home Video

THOUSANDS CHEER (1943)
"The Joint Is Really Jumpin' in Carnegie Hall"

This was MGM's morale boosting, World War II effort, different from Irving Berlin's 1933 Broadway revue *As Thousands Cheer*. It starred Kathryn Grayson and Gene Kelly, and featured a star-filled finale. Judy Garland performed "The Joint Is Really Jumpin' in Carnegie Hall," which was actually written by Roger Edens. He put the names of Martin and Blane on it because he thought he had borrowed part of it from their song "The Three B's."

Film premiere: New York, September 1943 / Los Angeles, December 1943 (126 minutes)
VHS: Warner Studios

BROADWAY RHYTHM (1944)
"Brazilian Boogie" (music & lyrics: Hugh Martin with Ralph Blane)

A backstage story about producing a musical on "The Great White Way," this MGM movie musical was a vehicle for numerous entertainers to show off their talents. Lena Horne performed the Carmen Miranda inspired "Brazilian Boogie," a song that cited its heritage as 'samba' and 'swing.'

Film premiere: January 1944 (115 minutes)
CD: *Lena Horne At M-G-M: Ain't It The Truth*, Turner Classic Movies Music
VHS: Turner Home Video

L to R: Hugh Martin, Judy Garland and Bing Crosby rehearse before a May 1944 radio broadcast of *MAIL CALL!*
The song "Connecticut" was written for Maj. Meredith Willson, music director and host for the Armed Forces Radio Service, who solicited songs about the States of the Union and was premiered by singer Connie Haines in June of '44. Garland and Crosby would perform the song on the *Philco Radio Time* program in February of '47.

Connecticut

Words and Music by
HUGH MARTIN and RALPH BLANE

23

26

MEET ME IN ST. LOUIS (1944, 1989)

Martin and Blane's original score and their adaptation of American folk songs captured turn-of-the-century St. Louis at the time of the 1904 World's Fair. Based on Sally Benson's writings, the MGM movie featured legendary performances and production values. Since the 1944 film, *Meet Me in St. Louis* has been produced as a television special in 1959 by CBS, on stage in 1960 at the St. Louis Municipal Opera, as a television series in 1966 by ABC, and on Broadway in 1989. "The Trolley Song" received an Academy Award nomination for Best Song in 1944 while "Have Yourself a Merry Little Christmas" has become a holiday standard. In 2004, the American Film Institute named both songs to its list of top 100 movie songs of all time.

Film premiere: St. Louis & New York, November 1944
(113 minutes)
Music & lyrics: Hugh Martin & Ralph Blane
Screenplay: Irving Brecher & Fred Finklehoffe
(from *The Kensington Stories* by Sally Benson)
Producer: Arthur Freed (MGM)
Director: Vincente Minnelli
Choreographer: Charles Walters
Music Director: George Stoll
Orchestrations: Roger Edens & Conrad Salinger
Photography: George Folsey (Technicolor)
Film Editor: Albert Akst
Art Directors: Cedric Gibbons & Lemuel Ayers
Costumes: Irene Sharaff

Judy Garland

Cast: Judy Garland *(Esther Smith)*; Margaret O'Brien *("Tootie" Smith)*; Mary Astor *(Anna Smith,* vocal by Rose Paidar and Eileen Wood*)*; Lucille Bremer *(Rose Smith)*; Leon Ames *(Alonzo Smith,* vocal by Arthur Freed*)*; Tom Drake *(John Truitt)*; Marjorie Main *(Katie)*; Harry Davenport *(Grandpa)*; June Lockhart *(Lucille Ballard)*; Henry H. Daniels, Jr. *(Lon Smith, Jr.)*; Joan Carroll *(Agnes Smith)*; Hugh Marlowe *(Col. Darly)*; Chill Wills *(Mr. Neeley)*; Robert Sully *(Warren Sheffield)*

Songs (by Martin unless noted): Meet Me in St. Louis, Louis (Kerry Mills & Andrew Sterling); The Boy Next Door; Skip to My Lou (traditional, this vocal arrangement was first recorded by The Martins in 1941); Under the Bamboo Tree (J. Rosamond Johnson & Bob Cole); I Was Drunk Last Night (trad.); Over the Bannister (trad.); The Trolley Song; You and I (Nacio Herb Brown & Arthur Freed); Have Yourself a Merry Little Christmas

CD: MGM (Soundtrack)
DVD: Warner Home Video

Hugh Martin (center) with Debby Boone and Stuart Larson from the 1991 National Tour of *Meet Me in St. Louis*

Broadway run: November 2, 1989 – July 10, 1990
(George Gershwin Theatre, 252 performances)
Music & lyrics: Hugh Martin & Ralph Blane
Book: Hugh Wheeler (from the writings of Sally Benson & the MGM film)
Producers: Brickhill-Burke Productions, Christopher Seabrooke & EPI Products
Director: Louis Burke
Choreographer: Joan Brickhill ("Ice" choreography by Michael Tokar)
Musical Director: Bruce Pomahac
Orchestrations: Michael Gibson (Dance arrangements by James Raitt)
Scenery and costumes: Keith Anderson
Lighting: Ken Billington

Cast: Betty Garrett *(Katie)*; George Hearn *(Mr. Alonzo Smith)*; Charlotte Moore *(Mrs. Smith)*; Milo O'Shea *(Grandpa Prophater)*; Donna Kane *(Esther Smith)*; Courtney Peldon *("Tootie" Smith)*; Karen Culliver *(Lucille Ballard)*; Rachael Graham *(Agnes Smith)*; Shauna Hicks *(Eve Finley)*; Brian Jay *(Randy Travis)*; Juliet Lambert *(Rose Smith)*; Craig A. Meyer *(Clinton A. Badger)*; Michael O'Steen *(Lon Smith)*; Peter Reardon *(Warren Sheffield)*; Naomi Reddin *(Ida Boothby)*; Gordon Stanley *(Dr. Bond)*; Gregg Whitney *(Douglas Moore)*; Jason Workman *(John Truitt)*; Jim Semmelman *(Motorman)*

Songs (by Martin unless noted): Meet Me in St. Louis (Mills & Sterling); The Boy Next Door (I Happen to Love You- interpolated from *Hans Brinker...*); Be Anything but a Girl*; Skip to My Lou (trad.); Under the Bamboo Tree (Johnson & Cole); Banjos; Ghosties and Ghoulies and Things that Go Bump in the Night*; Halloween Ballet*; Wasn't It Fun?; The Trolley Song; Ice* (from *Hans Brinker...*); A Raving Beauty*; A Touch of the Irish*; A Day in New York; The Ball*; Diamonds in the Starlight*; Have Yourself a Merry Little Christmas; Paging Mister Sousa*; Whenever I'm with You**; You'll Hear a Bell**; Over the Bannister (trad.)**; What's His Name?**; You Are for Loving***

　　　　*deleted from the 1991 National tour version
　　　　**added to the 1991 National tour version
　　　　***cited by Alec Wilder in his book *American Popular Song* as '...among the best theatre ballads ever written'

CD: DRG (Original Broadway Cast)

THE BOY NEXT DOOR

Words and Music by
HUGH MARTIN and RALPH BLANE

30

Have Yourself
a Merry Little Christmas
(Have Yourself a Blessed Little Christmas)

*Sacred Lyrics by
HUGH MARTIN and JOHN FRICKE

Words and Music by
HUGH MARTIN and RALPH BLANE

THE TROLLEY SONG

Words and Music by
HUGH MARTIN and RALPH BLANE

Astor Theatre marquee of the film *Meet Me in St. Louis*

L to R: Lucille Bremer, Leon Ames, Mary Astor, Joan Carroll, Vincente Minnelli, Judy Garland, Arthur Freed, Harry Davenport, Margaret O'Brien, Henry H. Daniels, Jr. from the MGM film *Meet Me in St. Louis*

L to R: Jeanne Crain, Ed Wynn, Myrna Loy, Walter Pidgeon, Jane Powell and Tab Hunter from the CBS broadcast of *Meet Me in St. Louis*

You Are for Loving

Words and Music by
HUGH MARTIN and RALPH BLANE

You'll Hear a Bell

Words and Music by
HUGH MARTIN and RALPH BLANE

50

Diamonds in the Starlight

Words and Music by
HUGH MARTIN and RALPH BLANE

ABBOTT AND COSTELLO IN HOLLYWOOD (1945)

"Fun on the Wonderful Midway" (music & lyrics: Hugh Martin with Ralph Blane)

After Hugh Martin went into the Army in 1944, Ralph Blane was assigned to this MGM picture featuring comedians Bud Abbott and Lou Costello. Wanting to keep the team of Martin and Blane intact, Ralph put Hugh's name on many of the film's songs. "Fun on the Wonderful Midway" is the only song Hugh wrote, though the lyric was re-written by Ralph to fit the script.

Film release: August 1945 (83 minutes)
CD: Rhino Handmade (4 songs from this film are included as extra tracks on the *Best Foot Forward* soundtrack.)
VHS: Warner Studios

ZIEGFELD FOLLIES (1945)

"Love" (music & lyrics: Hugh Martin with Ralph Blane)

Filmed in the style of an opulent Ziegfeld revue with the vast resources of MGM, this lavish movie was filled with immense talent in front of and behind the camera. If not cut from the film, "Pass that Peace Pipe" was to be sung by any number of stars including Judy Garland, Fred Astaire, Lucille Ball, Gene Kelly, June Allyson and/or Robert Walker. The Martin and Blaine song featured in the movie was "Love," performed by Lena Horne.

Film premiere: Boston, August 1945 / New York, March 1946 (110 minutes)
CD: Rhino (Soundtrack)
VHS: Warner Studios

L to R: Tom Drake, Margaret O'Brien and Judy Garland prepare for the December 1946 CBS broadcast of *The Lux Radio Theatre.* An hour-long version of *Meet Me in St. Louis* was presented with Garland performing songs from the film.

GOOD NEWS (1947)

"Pass that Peace Pipe" (music & lyrics: Hugh Martin with Roger Edens and Ralph Blane)

Twenty years after this DeSylva, Brown and Henderson show ran on Broadway, MGM produced the musical in Technicolor, the first film effort being a black-and-white version in 1930. While keeping a half dozen of the original songs and the plot's carefree collegiate optimism, new numbers were added to the story, including the imaginative "Pass that Peace Pipe." The song earned the authors an Academy Award Nomination for Best Song in 1947.

Film premiere: New York, December 1947 (92 minutes)
CD: Rhino Handmade (Soundtrack)
DVD: Warner Home Video

Pass that Peace Pipe

Words and Music by ROGER EDENS,
HUGH MARTIN and RALPH BLANE

59

Love

Words and Music by
HUGH MARTIN and RALPH BLANE

64

THE HUGH MARTIN SHOW (1948)

Both George Abbott and Harold Prince wrote and directed this short-lived television program, which took place on a set resembling Hugh's living room. Even with the talents of Kaye Ballard, Joan McCracken and Butterfly McQueen, only three episodes were aired by NBC.

LOOK, MA, I'M DANCIN'! (1948)

With *Look, Ma, I'm Dancin'!*, Hugh Martin was reunited with *Best Foot Forward* producer/director George Abbott and leading lady Nancy Walker, in this, his first solo effort as composer/lyricist. Based on an idea by choreographer Jerome Robbins, the show was about the on and off stage comedic antics of a dilettante heiress who wants to dance professionally, has no talent, so funds the tour of a ballet company. *Look, Ma, I'm Dancin'!* was revived in 2000 by Musicals Tonight!, a theatre company dedicated to the revival of 'neglected' musicals.

Broadway run: January 29, 1948 – July 10, 1948
(Adelphi Theatre, 188 performances)
Music & lyrics: Hugh Martin
Book: Jerome Lawrence & Robert E. Lee
Producer: George Abbott
Directors: George Abbott & Jerome Robbins
Choreographer: Jerome Robbins
Musical Director: Pembroke Davenport
Orchestrations: Don Walker
Scenery: Oliver Smith
Costumes: John Pratt

Nancy Walker

Cast: Nancy Walker *(Lily Malloy)*; Sandra Deel *(Suzy)*; Virginia Gorski *(Snow White)*; Robert H. Harris *(F. Plancek)*; Harold Lang *(Eddie Winkler)*; Don Liberto *(Wotan)*; Alexander March *(Vladimir Luboff)*; Alice Pearce *(Dusty Lee)*; Tommy Rall *(Tommy)*; Janet Reed *(Ann Bruce)*; Katharine Sergava *(Tanya Drinskaya)*; Loren Welch *(Larry)*; James Lane *(Mr. Gleeb)*; Eddie Hodge *(Mr. Ferbish)*; Raul Celada *(Tanya's Partner)*; Dean Campbell *(Bell Boy)*; Dan Sattler *(Stage Manager)*

Songs: Gotta Dance; I'm the First Girl in the Second Row in the Third Scene of the Fourth Number; I'm Not So Bright; I'm Tired of Texas; Tiny Room; The Little Boy Blues; Mademoiselle Marie (ballet music by Trude Rittman); Jazz; The New Look; If You'll Be Mine; Pajama Dance; Shauny O'Shay; Pas de Deux from *Swan Lake* (Tchaikovsky); The Two of Us; Let's Do a Ballet*; Wonderful, Wonderful Love*; Horrible, Horrible Love**; All My Life***

*dropped from the Broadway production
**dropped from B'way / added to Musicals Tonight!
***added to the Musicals Tonight! production

CDs: Decca (Original Broadway Cast)
Original Cast (Musicals Tonight! Cast)

GOTTA DANCE

Words and Music by
HUGH MARTIN

Rhythmically—With Energy

(* Alternate lyric written by Mr. Martin for a benefit concert)

I'm the First Girl
(In the Second Row in the Third Scene of the Fourth Number)

Words and Music by
HUGH MARTIN

Moderato

March Tempo

Refrain

sempre staccato

wise. You can spot me if you mem-o - rize this dai - ly tale of woe:_____ I'm the fame:_____ I'm the

first girl in the se - cond row in the third scene of the fourth num-ber in
first girl in the se - cond row in the third scene of the fourth num-ber in

fifth po - si - tion at ten o' - clock on the nose. I'm the
fifth po - si - tion; you'll won - der why you came. I'm the

nique of Tou - mon-o-va,_____ and as for Al-ex-an-dra Da-

nil-o-va,_____ I know I'll nev-er make a shle-meil-o-va._____

- For peo-ple who have al - rea-dy seen a,_____ I'll

nev-er be an-oth - er Zor-i-na._____ I can't re-place Pav-

Tiny Room

Words and Music by
HUGH MARTIN

Refrain (*slowly*)

GRANDMA MOSES (1950)

Hugh Martin wrote the music for Jerome Hill's Academy Award nominated movie about the primitive-style artist at home with her paintings. The film score, orchestrated by Alec Wilder, is comprised of ten movements: "Cambridge Valley"; "Whistle Stop"; "Anna Mary"; "Sugaring Off"; "Sewing"; "Children's Children's Children"; "Winter in Hoosick Falls"; "Pioneer Stock"; "Lullaby"; "Christmas" (Pastoral, Violin Solo and Music Box).

Film release: October 1950 (23 minutes) Falcon Films
CD: *The Grandma Moses Suite/Blues Opera*, DRG

MAKE A WISH (1951)

Ferenc Molnár's play *The Good Fairy* had previously been seen on stage and in the cinema. *Make a Wish* was the title for the musical adaptation and marked composer/lyricist Hugh Martin's second full Broadway score. With Paris as its location, the show featured lavish costumes and scenery, one of the costliest works produced on Broadway during that era, as well as the talents of leading-lady Nanette Fabray and choreographer Gower Champion.

New York run: April 18, 1951 – July 14, 1951
(Winter Garden Theatre, 102 performances)
Music & lyrics: Hugh Martin
Producers: Harry Rigby, Jule Styne
         & Alexander H. Cohen
Book: Preston Sturges
(based on *The Good Fairy* by Ferenc Molnár)
Director: John C. Wilson
Choreographer: Gower Champion
Musical Director: Milton Rosenstock
(Vocal direction by Buster Davis)
Orchestrations: Phil Lang & Allan Small
(Dance arrangements by Richard Pribor)
Scenery and costumes: Raoul Pène du Bois

Nanette Fabray

Cast: Nanette Fabray *(Janette)*; Melville Cooper *(Marius Frigo)*; Stephen Douglass *(Paul Dumont)*; Helen Gallagher *(Poupette)*; Harold Lang *(Ricky)*; Eda Heinemann *(Dr. Didier)*; Phil Leeds *(Dr. Francel)*; Howard Wendell *(Policeman/Sales Mgr.)*; Mary Finney *(The Madam)*; LeRoi Operti *(Felix Labiche)*; George Spelvin *(Old Gentleman)*

Songs: The Tour Must Go On; I Wanna Be Good 'n Bad; The Time Step (dance); You're Just What I Was Warned About; Who Gives a Sou; Hello, Hello, Hello; Tonight You Are in Paree; When Does This Feeling Go Away?; Suits Me Fine; Student's Ball (ballet); Paris, France; That Face; Make a Wish; I'll Never Make a Frenchman out of You; Over and Over; The Sale (ballet); The Shopping List* (a.k.a. The Pâtisserie); They're Not in a Class with You; Take Me Back to Texas with You

       *dropped from the Broadway production

CD: Sepia (Original Broadway Cast)

What I Was Warned About

Lyric and Music by
HUGH MARTIN

Over and Over

Lyric and Music by
HUGH MARTIN

Chorus (*Very fast*)

O - ver and o - ver I ask my - self What is this mag-ic you brew. _____ With the sea so full of fish, Why should I wish for you? _____ O - ver and o - ver I ask my - self When I'll dis - cov - er a clue. _____

WHEN DOES THIS FEELING GO AWAY?

Lyric and Music by
HUGH MARTIN

Chorus (*Not too slowly*)

THE SHOPPING LIST
(THE PÂTISSERIE)

Lyric and Music by
HUGH MARTIN

Moderato, with Expression

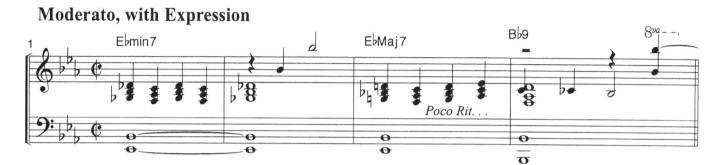

Verse
Rubato (Not Too Slow)

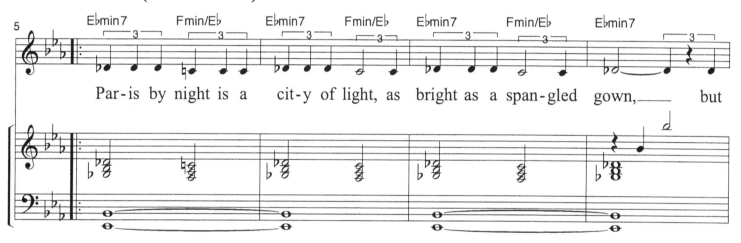

Par-is by night is a cit-y of light, as bright as a span-gled gown,____ but

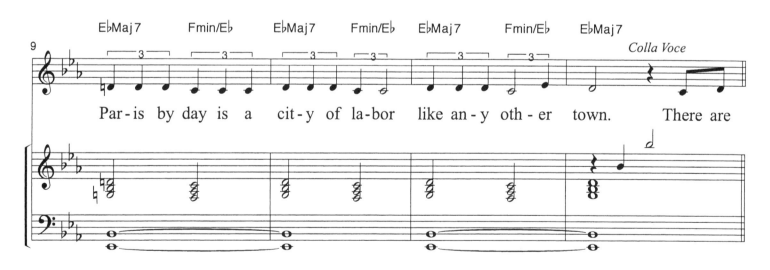

Par-is by day is a cit-y of la-bor like an-y oth-er town. There are

*Pronounced "Robaire"

"The Shopping List" is a new title for the song "The Pâtisserie." It was originally intended to have been sung by Janette, our heroine, in counterpart to the love song "When Does This Feeling Go Away?", being sung to her by Paul, our hero. It was to have been the big moment of the show. However, Irving Berlin had just opened *Call Me Madam* a few days ahead of our show! We heard by the grapevine that Irving had given Ethel Merman and Russell Nype a duet called "You're Not Sick, You're Just in Love." We hastily deleted our song because the device was identical, but in all fairness, I have to admit that Berlin originated the idea decades before with a clever little tune called "Play a Simple Melody." (Hugh)

PENNY PLAIN (1951)

In 1951, producer Laurier Lister created an intimate revue, *Penny Plain*, for the London stage. Singer Elisabeth Welch performed "The Pâtisserie," which was cut from *Make a Wish*, and "I've Been in a Daze for Days," a song by Hugh Martin and Timothy Gray.

London Run: June 1951
(St. Martin's Theatre)

LOVE FROM JUDY (1952)

Based on Jean Webster's novel *Daddy Long Legs*, Hugh Martin's longest running musical was created with Timothy Gray for London's West End. Set in 1903 New Orleans, it is a 'Cinderella' tale of an orphan named Judy Abbott. *Love from Judy* received its American premiere in 1957 at the University of Alabama-Birmingham with Mr. Martin's sister, Ellen, playing the title role. A New York City performance of the show was produced by Musicals Tonight! in 2003.

Jean Carson

West End run: September 25, 1952 – February 20, 1954
(Saville Theatre, 594 performances)
Music & lyrics: Hugh Martin & Jack (Timothy) Gray
Book: Eric Maschwitz & Jean Webster
(based on *Daddy Long Legs* by Jean Webster)
Producer: Emile Littler
Director: Charles Hickman
Choreographer: Pauline Grant
Musical Director: Philip Martell
Orchestrations: Phil Green
Scenery and costumes: Berkeley Stucliffe

Cast: Jean Carson *(Jerusha 'Judy' Abbott)*; Barbara Deeks *(Sadie Kate)*; Pixie Murphy *(Gladiola Murphy)*; Moiya Kelly *(Mamie)*; Heather Lee *(Loretta)*; Mary Marvin *(Mrs. Lippett/Mrs. Pendleton)*; Linda Gray *(Mrs. Grace Pritchard)*; Vincent Larson *(Cyrus Wykoff/Walters)*; Joss Clewes *(Senator Parsons)*; Bill O'Connor *(Jervis Pendleton)*; Audrey Freeman *(Julia Pendleton)*; June Whitfield *(Sally McBride)*; Johnny Brandon *(Jimmy McBride)*; William Greene *(Gordon McClintock)*; Adelaide Hall *("Butterfly")*; Jeanette Landis *(Mary Lou Wagner)*; James Ansley *(Wilberforce)*; Anne Foley *(Louie Jean)*; David Karry *(Don Mize)*; Rex Reid *(Ballet Jervis)*; Irene Claire *(Ballet Judy)*; Frances Pidgeon *(Ballet Magnolia)*; Thane Bettany *(Capt. Le Valier)*

Songs (by Martin unless noted): Mardi Gras; I Never Dream When I'm Asleep; It's Great to Be an Orphan (lyrics by Gray); Goin' Back to School (lyrics-Gray); Dumb-Dumb-Dumb; It's Better Rich (lyrics-Gray); Daddy Long-Legs (lyrics- Gray); Love from Judy (lyrics-Gray); A Touch of Voodoo; Here We Are; Go and Get Your Old Banjo (lyrics-Gray); Kind to Animals; Ain't Gonna Marry (based on traditional American folk songs); My True Love; What Do I See in You? (lyrics-Gray/dance arrangement-Walter Crisham); Ballet (music-Phil Green)

CD: Sepia (Original London Cast)

I Never Dream When I'm Asleep

Music by HUGH MARTIN
Lyrics by JACK GRAY

ATHENA (1954)

The production number "I Never Felt Better" summed up the film *Athena*, an Eisenhower-era movie filled with music and muscle. Jane Powell (Athena) and Debbie Reynolds (Minerva) starred as sisters who fall in love with a lawyer (Purdom) and a singer (Damone), respectively, instead of following the wishes of their health-minded father. The film included Steve Reeves, Mr. Universe, who attempted to win the heart and body of the title character. The song "The Boy Next Door" was interpolated into the score as "The Girl Next Door."

Film release: November 1954 (95 minutes)
Music & lyrics: Hugh Martin with Ralph Blane
Screenplay: William Ludwig & Leonard Spigelgass
Producer: Joe Pasternak (MGM)
Director: Richard Thorpe
Choreographer: Valerie Bettis
Musical Director: George Stoll
Orchestrations: Robert Van Eps
Recording Director: Wesley C. Miller
Cinematography: Robert H. Planck (Technicolor)
Film Editor: Gene Ruggiero
Art Directors: Cedric Gibbons & Paul Groesse
Set Decoration: Henry Grace & Edwin B. Willis
Costumes: Walter Plunkett & Helen Rose
Makeup/Hair: William Tuttle/Sidney Guilaroff

Cast: Jane Powell *(Athena Mulvain)*; Debbie Reynolds *(Minerva Mulvain)*; Virginia Gibson *(Niobe Mulvain)*; Nancy Kilgas *(Aphrodite Mulvain)*; Dolores Starr *(Calliope Mulvain)*; Jane Fischer *(Medea Mulvain)*; Cecile Rogers *(Ceres Mulvain)*; Edmund Purdom *(Adam Calhorn Shaw,* vocal by Victor Marchese*)*; Vic Damone *(Johnny Nyle)*; Louis Calhern *(Grandpa Ulysses Mulvain)*; Evelyn Varden *(Grandma Salome Mulvain)*; Linda Christian *(Beth Hallson)*; Ray Collins *(Mr. Tremaine)*; Carl Benton Reid *(Mr. Griswalde)*; Howard Wendell *(Mr. Grenville)*; Henry Nakamura *(Roy, Adam's Houseboy)*; Steve Reeves *(Ed Perkins)*; Kathleen Freeman *(Miss Seely)*; Richard Sabre *(Bill Nichols)*

Songs (by Martin unless noted): Imagine; Love Can Change the Stars; Venezia; Vocalize; I Never Felt Better; The Girl Next Door; Chancun Le Suit (Donizetti); Webson's Meat Jingle (Jeff Alexander & George Stoll)

CD: Rhino Handmade (Soundtrack)
VHS: Turner Home Video

L to R: Debbie Reynolds, Hugh Martin, Jane Powell, Ralph Blane

Love Can Change the Stars

Words and Music by
HUGH MARTIN and RALPH BLANE

111

112

THE GIRL RUSH

(1955)

Set primarily in Las Vegas, *The Girl Rush* starred Broadway and Hollywood veteran Rosalind Russell. She mistakenly believed herself to be part owner of the Flamingo Hotel, eventually becoming involved with its real owner, Fernando Lamas, while Eddie Albert and Gloria DeHaven were paired as the supporting romantic leads.

Film release: August 1955 (84 minutes)
Music & lyrics: Hugh Martin with Ralph Blane
Screenplay: Robert Pirosh & Jerome Davis
(based on a story by Henry & Phoebe Ephron)
Producer: Frederick Brisson & Robert Alton (Paramount)
Director: Robert Pirosh
Choreography: Robert Alton
Musical score: Spencer-Hagen
Cinematography: William H. Daniels
(Vistavision/Technicolor)
Film Editor: William Hornbeck
Art Directors: Malcolm C. Bert & Hal Pereira
Set Decoration: Sam Comer & Darrell Silvera
Costumes: Edith Head
Makeup: Wally Westmore

Fernando Lamas and Rosalind Russell

Cast: Rosalind Russell *(Kim Halliday)*; Fernando Lamas *(Victor Monte)*; Eddie Albert *(Elliot Atterbury)*; Gloria DeHaven *(Taffy Tremaine)*; Marion Lorne *(Aunt Clara)*; James Gleason *(Ether Ferguson)*; Robert Fosrtier *(Pete Tremaine)*

Songs (by Martin unless noted): An Occasional Man; At Last We're Alone; Out-of-Doors; Birmin'ham; Homesick Hillbilly; Champagne; Choose Your Partner; Take a Chance; The Girl Rush; I Take a Dim View of the West (instrumental); Miss Jemima Walks By (Johnny Burke & James Van Heusen)

An Occasional Man

Words and Music by
HUGH MARTIN and RALPH BLANE

116

THE GIRL MOST LIKELY (1957)

> *The Girl Most Likely* was the last project on which Hugh Martin and Ralph Blane collaborated as well as the last film produced by the RKO studio. It revolved around Jane Powell and the three men to whom she became engaged. "Balboa" and "All the Colors of the Rainbow" featured athletic choreography by Gower Champion.

Film premiere: Los Angeles, December 1957 (98 minutes)
Music & lyrics: Hugh Martin with Ralph Blane
Screenplay: Devery Freeman
(based on the screenplay *Tom, Dick And Harry* by Paul Jarrico)
Producer: Stanley Rubin (RKO)
Director: Mitchell Leisen
Choreography: Gower Champion
Musical Director: Nelson Riddle
Cinematography: Robert H. Planck (Technicolor)
Film Editors: Doane Harrison & Harry Marker
Art Directors: Albert S. D'Agostino & George W. Davis
Set Decoration: Eli Benneche
Costumes: Renié
Makeup/Hair: Harry Maret, Jr./Larry Germain

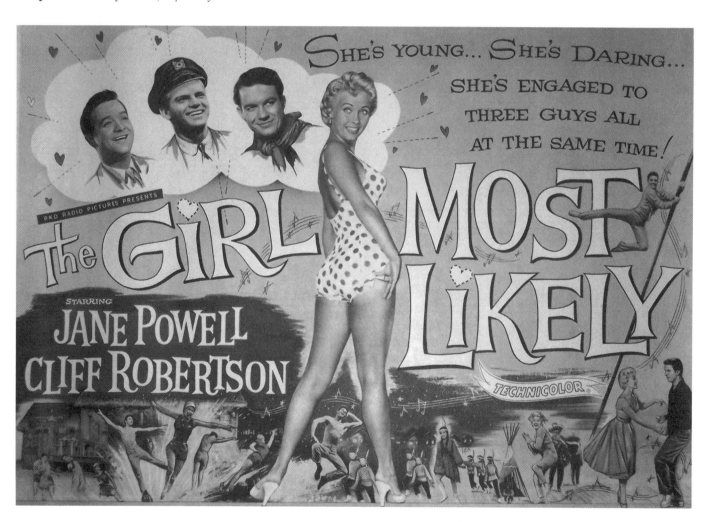

Cast: Jane Powell *(Dodie)*; Cliff Robertson *(Pete, vocal by Hal Derwin)*; Keith Andes *(Neil Patterson, Jr.)*; Kaye Ballard *(Marge)*; Tommy Noonan *(Buzz)*; Una Merkel *(Mom)*; Kelly Brown *(Sam Kelsey)*; Judy Nugent *(Pauline)*; Frank Cady *(Pop)*

Songs (by Martin unless noted): Balboa; I Like the Feeling; I Don't Know What I Want; My Song; Keeping Up with the Jones; Travelogue (part of Balboa); Crazy Horse; All the Colors of the Rainbow; The Girl Most Likely (Bob Russell & Nelson Riddle); Wedding Fantasy (Richard Pribor)

CD: DRG (Soundtrack)
VHS: Interglobal Home Video

I Like the Feeling

Words and Music by
HUGH MARTIN and RALPH BLANE

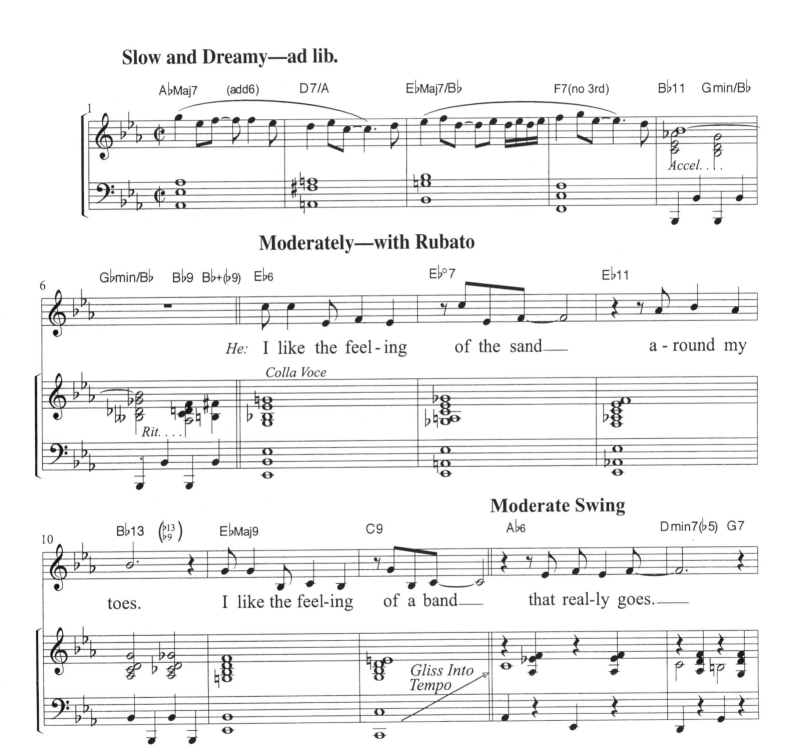

122

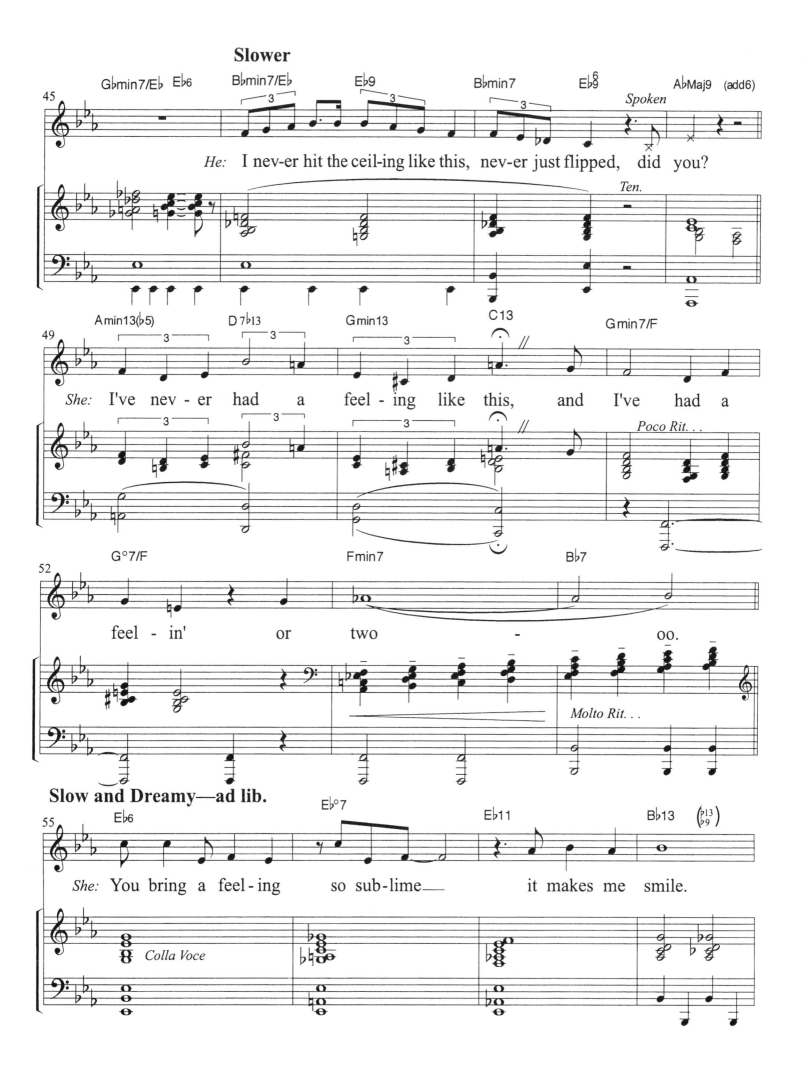

123

THE PATRICE MUNSEL SHOW (1957-58)

"Breezy and Easy" (music & lyrics: Hugh Martin)

> Metropolitan opera soprano Patrice Munsel was the host of her own primetime show for a season on ABC. Hugh Martin wrote "Breezy and Easy" as the theme song for this musical variety series that also featured the Martins Quartet (Hugh Martin, Ralph Blane, Jo Jean Rogers and Phyllis Rogers.)

Television broadcast: October 18, 1957 – June 13, 1958 (ABC, 30 minutes)

HANS BRINKER OR THE SILVER SKATES (1958)

> The novel about a noble Dutch boy was created by the American writer Mary Mapes Dodge. Showcasing the talents of skater Dick Button as well as actors Tab Hunter, Peggy King and Basil Rathbone, the television script was created by *Meet Me in St. Louis* author Sally Benson. Hugh Martin adapted two songs from *Hans Brinker...* for the 1989 Broadway version of *Meet Me in St. Louis*- "I Happen to Love You," which lengthened "The Boy Next Door" and "Ice," which opened Act II.

Television broadcast: February 9, 1958
(*Hallmark Hall of Fame*, 90 minutes)
Music & lyrics: Hugh Martin
Teleplay: Sally Benson
(based on *Hans Brinker...* by Mary Mapes Dodge)
Producers: Mildred Freed Alberg & Paul Feigay (NBC)
Director: Sidney Lumet
Choreographer: John Butler
Music Director: Franz Allers
(Vocal arrangements by Buster Davis)
Orchestrations: Irwin Kostal
(Dance arrangements by John Morris)
Editor: Robert Hartung
Art Director: Jan Scott
Costumes: Noel Taylor
Lighting: William Knight

L to R: Dick Button, Peggy King, Tab Hunter

Cast: Tab Hunter *(Hans Brinker)*; Peggy King *(Rychie Van Gleck)*: Basil Rathbone *(Dr. Boekman)*; Jarmila Novotna *(Dame Brinker)*; Carmen Matthews *(Mevrouw Van Gleck)*; Dick Button *(Peter Van Gleck)*; Ellie Sommers *(Trinka)*; Paul Robertson *(Pote Van Gleck)*; Ralph Roberts *(Raff Brinker)*; John Fielder *(Vollenhoven)*; Jana Pierce *(Lucretia)*; Blair Heimbach *(Carl)*; Martha Greenhouse *(Housekeeper)*; Florence Anglin *(Hilda)*; Matt Crowley *(Old Man)*; Frances Gaar *(Nurse)*; Luke Halpin *(Boy)*

Songs: I Happen to Love You; I'm a Very Lucky Boy; Trinka, Brinka; A Job for Me; Ice; Clop, Clop, Clop; The More the Merrier; Hello Springtime

LP: Dot (Original Television Cast)

I Happen to Love You

By HUGH MARTIN

HIGH SPIRITS

(1964)

> Noël Coward's comedy *Blithe Spirit* was the basis for the musical *High Spirits* by Martin and Gray. The unusual plot of ghosts, marriage and mayhem was shepherded by Coward and starred the larger-than-life actress Beatrice Lillie. Opening in 1964, it surpassed the Broadway run of *Best Foot Forward* and was produced in London's West End later that year, playing 93 performances. In 1964, Hugh Martin and Timothy Gray earned Tony nominations for Best Composer, Lyricist and Adaptation.

New York run: April 7, 1964 – February 27, 1965
(Alvin Theatre, 375 performances)
Music, lyrics & book: Hugh Martin & Timothy Gray
(based on *Blithe Spirit* by Noël Coward)
Producers: Lester Osterman, Robert Fletcher
        & Richard Horner
Director: Noël Coward
(Gower Champion uncredited)
Choreographer: Danny Daniels
Musical Director: Fred Werner
Orchestrations: Harry Zimmerman
(Dance music by William Goldenberg)
Scenery & costumes: Robert Fletcher
(additional costumes by Valentina)
Lighting: Jules Fisher

L to R: Tammy Grimes, Beatrice Lillie, Edward Woodward

Cast: Beatrice Lillie *(Madame Arcati)*; Tammy Grimes *(Elvira)*; Edward Woodward *(Charles Condomine)*; Louise Troy *(Ruth Condomine)*; Carol Arthur *(Edith)*; Gene Castle *(Rupert)*; Margaret Hall *(Mrs. Bradman)*; Beth Howland *(Beth)*; Lawrence Keith *(Dr. Bradman)*; Robert Lenn *(Bob)*

Songs (by Hugh Martin unless noted): Was She Prettier Than I? (lyrics by Martin & Gray); The Bicycle Song (lyrics-Martin & Gray); You'd Better Love Me (lyrics-Martin & Gray); Where Is the Man I Married? (lyrics-Martin & Gray); The Sandwich Man (lyrics-Gray); Go into Your Trance (lyrics-Gray); Forever and a Day; Something Tells Me; I Know Your Heart (lyrics-Martin & Gray); Faster than Sound (lyrics-Martin & Gray); If I Gave You; Talking to You (lyrics-Martin & Gray); Home Sweet Heaven (lyrics-Gray); The Exorcism (lyrics-Gray); Something Is Coming to Tea (lyrics-Gray); What in the World Did You Want? (lyrics-Gray); Is There Anybody There (lyrics-Gray); The Society (lyrics-Gray); Flowers (lyrics-Gray); Have an Umbrella (lyrics-Gray)

CDs: MCA (Original Broadway Cast)
      DRG (Original London Cast)

Home Sweet Heaven

Words and Music by
HUGH MARTIN and TIMOTHY GRAY

131

fun when Jul - ius Cae - sar___ Proust and St. The - re - sa___
real - ly bowl you o - ver___ Watch - ing Ca - sa - no - va___

drop - in for a cup of tea. Dis - rael - i's
try - ing to flirt with Ger - trude Stein. *(She's a gas, is a gas.)* De - li - lah's

dar - ling___ and Ho - mer's heart - y___ And Joan of
drea - ry___ but Sam - son's hand - some_ And with his

134

"HOME SWEET HEAVEN" ENCORE CHORUS

There's Mussolini draped in a sari,
Mad as a hatter, like a fatter Mata Hari.
He splits a kipper with Jack the Ripper
In my Home Sweet Heaven.

We often dine on divine spaghetti
In a little fun place, run by Sacco and Vanzetti.
Where I sip vino with Valentino
In my Home Sweet Heaven.

I miss Tallulah dramatizing, Judy vocalizing,
(spoken) Joan Crawford and her motherly advice.
And when I waltz with Leslie Howard, or laugh with Noël Coward,
Then it's really paradise.

Lady Godiva is going steady
With old King Ethelred who's hardly ever ready.
They share a chalet with Walter Raleigh and his good Queen Bessie,
It's rather messy.

I miss the concerts by Puccini and Rossini,
And even that old chicken, Tetrazzini.
I'm homesick for my Home Sweet 1-2 Heaven,
And it's a gas, it's a gas, it's a gas,
I'm homesick for my Home Sweet Heaven.

Hugh Martin and Timothy Gray

Author's Note: I can never say "this is how I write," because I seldom do it the same way twice. Ralph Blane and I wrote individually, that is, when I worked on a song, I did both music and lyrics, as did he. Writing *Look, Ma, I'm Dancin'!* by myself was fulfilling artistically but lonely as all get out. During *Make a Wish*, Timothy Gray was irreplaceable, feeding me many valuable ideas that I polished and took credit for (at his insistence). This led to *Love From Judy*, in which I did the music, and Timothy and I collaborated on the lyrics. In the early 1960s, I worked with Marshall Barer, a poet of enormous distinction. His lyrics were so brilliant that I didn't tamper with them. But none of this quite satisfied my artistic soul. What to do? I'm happy to say that Providence provided the answer with *High Spirits*. Timothy's lyric and book writing had a new sophistication and wit, a result of his years living with one foot in New York and one foot in London. Our joint lyrics inspired me to write music at the top of my form. (Hugh)

If I Gave You

Words and Music by
HUGH MARTIN and TIMOTHY GRAY

138

You'd Better Love Me

Words and Music by
HUGH MARTIN and TIMOTHY GRAY

141

Hugh Martin composing *High Spirits*

HERE COME THE DREAMERS

Music: Hugh Martin / **Lyrics:** Marshall Barer

Unproduced until a 1998 concert version in Los Angeles, this work was written in the early 1960s for Kathryn Grayson and Liza Minnelli. A show business 'back story' set on a Hollywood soundstage, it has also been titled *A Happy Lot, A Little Night Music* and *Music at Midnight*. The song "Wasn't It Romantic" is published in the collection *Michael Feinstein – Isn't It Romantic*.

TATTERED TOM

Music & lyrics: Hugh Martin

Unproduced, this musical was based on the 1871 novel *Tattered Tom or, The Story of a Street Arab* by Horatio Alger, a 'rags-to-riches' story of a girl named 'Tom.' Written in the late 1960s, two songs from the score, "A Day in New York" and "Whenever I'm with You," were adapted for the 1989 Broadway version of *Meet Me in St. Louis*. "Up to My Elbows" was adapted as "Up to My Eyebrows" for the 2004 York Theatre version of *Best Foot Forward*.

WEDDING DAY

Music & lyrics: Hugh Martin

Carson McCullers' 1946 novel *The Member of the Wedding* was a coming-of-age story concerning a 12-year-old Georgia girl named Frankie. The semi-autobiographical work was adapted into a play in 1950 and a film in 1952. Hugh Martin's musical version was presented as a showcase directed by Joshua Logan in Birmingham, Alabama in 1995.

On Such a Night As This

Lyric by MARSHALL BARER
Music by HUGH MARTIN

146

Gentle Jesus

Words and Music by
HUGH MARTIN

Slowly with movement

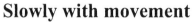

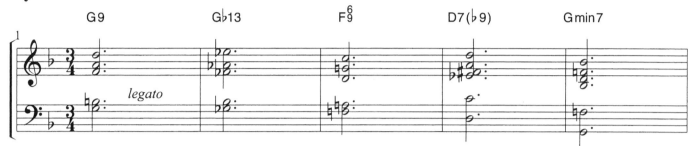

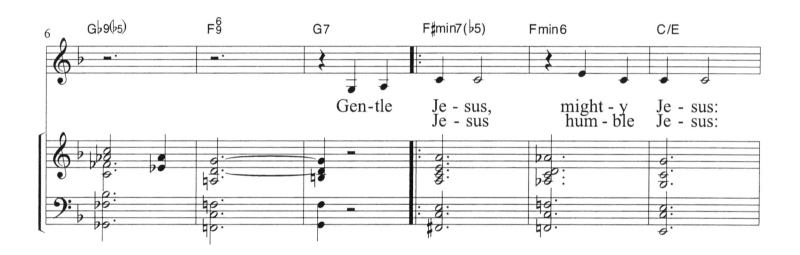

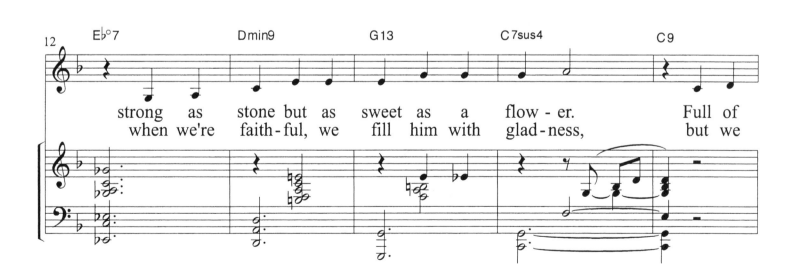

*Cue notes 2nd time

I Have Something to Say to You

Words and Music by
HUGH MARTIN

156

INDIVIDUAL SONGS

"It's Christmas Time All over the World" was written in the mid-1960s and recorded by Sammy Davis, Jr. It can be heard on the recording *Christmas with the Rat Pack*, CD: Capitol, 2002.

"Thanksgiving Should Be Ev'ry Day" was completed recently by Hugh Martin and is published for the first time in this songbook. With its original harmonies and timeless sentiment, it will surely join "Have Yourself a Merry Little Christmas" as a favorite holiday standard.

"Goodbye Today, Hello Tonight" was an original song that completed a private recording of 'standards' by Simone Levitt, wife of Levittown creator Bill Levitt. Both lyrically romantic and musically effervescent, it was written especially for Mrs. Levitt.

"The Story of My Life" is a simple one. I have had a most felicitous and blest life, and I was reflecting on that fact one afternoon in Newbury Park, California. "I've laughed a lot," I thought to myself, "and I've cried a lot." Indeed, my subconscious began to elaborate, everything I did, I did "a lot." I never did anything half-heartedly. By now, I was reaching for a ball-point pen and the lyrics were flowing almost faster than I could write them down. (Hugh)

SELECTED RECORDINGS

Three by Hugh Martin, LP: COL, 1954
Martin & Blane Sing Martin and Blane, CD: DRG, 1994
Michael Feinstein Sings The Hugh Martin Songbook, CD: Nonesuch, 1995
Marlene VerPlanck-You'd Better Love Me, CD: Audiophile, 1997
Judy Live at the Palace, CD: Howards International, 2001
Hugh Sings Martin, CD: PS Classics, 2005

Hugh Martin and Michael Feinstein

It's Christmas Time All over the World

Words and Music by
HUGH MARTIN

THANKSGIVING SHOULD BE EV'RY DAY

Words and Music by
HUGH MARTIN

Tempo Moderato

Refrain
Tempo Moderato

Goodbye Today, Hello Tonight

Words and Music by
HUGH MARTIN and TIMOTHY GRAY

Moderato — Not Too Slow

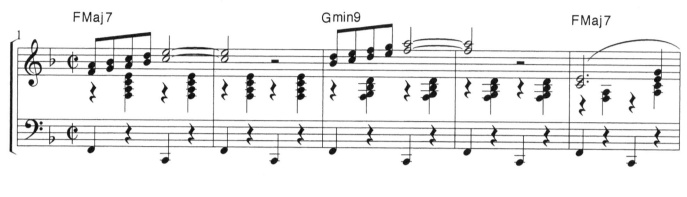

Good - bye to - day, hel -

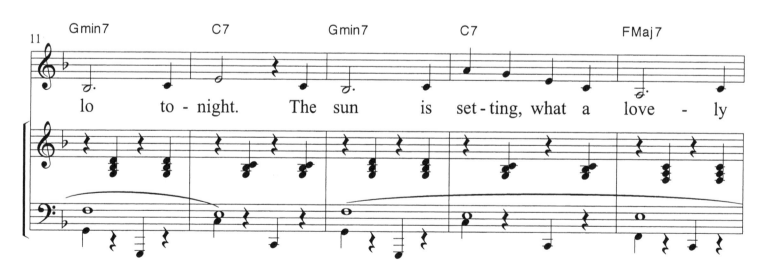

lo to - night.   The sun   is   set - ting, what a   love - ly

170

The Story of My Life

Words and Music by
HUGH MARTIN

Moderately—with Feeling

With Expression

Love was the thing I had the most of; my life was a cra-zy quilt. It

was-n't a life a girl could boast of, but I lived it to the hilt. I
(guy)

Chorus **Subtle Tango Tempo**

laughed a lot,_____ cried a lot._____ I failed a lot,____

____ but I tried a lot._____ Tired a lot, al-ways on the

174

VOCAL ARRANGEMENTS & DIRECTION

	STAGE	FILM
HOORAY FOR WHAT!	1937	
BOYS FROM SYRACUSE, THE	1938	
ONE FOR THE MONEY	1939	
STARS IN YOUR EYES	1939	
STREETS OF PARIS, THE	1939	
TOO MANY GIRLS	1939	1940
VERY WARM FOR MAY	1939	
DUBARRY WAS A LADY	1939	
LOUISIANA PURCHASE	1940	
WALK WITH MUSIC	1940	
CABIN IN THE SKY	1940	1943
PAL JOEY	1940	
HI YA, GENTLEMEN	1940	
PRESENTING LILY MARS		1943
GIRL CRAZY		1943
BAREFOOT BOY WITH CHECK	1947	
HIGH BUTTON SHOES	1947	
HEAVEN ON EARTH	1948	
AS THE GIRLS GO	1948	
GENTLEMEN PREFER BLONDES	1949	
WEST POINT STORY, THE		1950
JUDY GARLAND AT THE PALACE	1951	
TOP BANANA	1951	
MACAO		1952
HAZEL FLAGG	1953	
A STAR IS BORN		1954
ZIEGFELD FOLLIES OF 1956	1956	
TIMOTHY GRAY'S TABOO REVUE	1959	
LORELEI	1974	
GOOD NEWS!	1974	
SUGAR BABIES	1979	

Judy Garland and Hugh Martin relaxing from their 'two-a-day' show schedule at the Palace Theatre in 1951.